KEY

- Wildfl...................................... or and organi........................... blooms.
- Leaf at.............................. wildflower.
- Descriptions include important facts such as cluster shape, number of petals, or center color to help you quickly identify the species. Size information is sometimes included as well.
- Species marked with this icon ⓘ are introduced, non-native, and sometimes invasive.
- Species marked with either icon **S V** are a shrub or vine.
- Species marked with **A P B** are annual, perennial, or biennial, respectively. Some species can be more than one, depending on environment and growing conditions.

LEAF ATTACHMENT

Wildflower leaves attach to stems in different ways. The leaf icons next to the flowers show alternate, opposite, whorled, perfoliate, clasping, and basal attachments. Some wildflower plants have two or more types of leaf attachments.

 ALTERNATE leaves attach in an alternating pattern.

 OPPOSITE leaves attach directly opposite each other.

 BASAL leaves originate at the base of the plant and are usually grouped in pairs or in a rosette.

 PERFOLIATE leaves are stalkless and have a leaf base that completely surrounds the main stem.

 CLASPING leaves have no stalk, and the base partly surrounds the main stem.

 WHORLED leaves have three or more leaves that attach around the stem at the same point.

 CLUSTERED leaves originate from the same point on the stem.

 SPINES are leaves that take the form of sharp spines.

PARTS OF A FLOWER

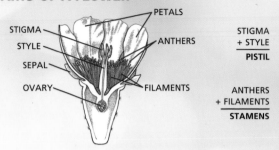

PETALS

STIGMA
STYLE
SEPAL
OVARY

ANTHERS

FILAMENTS

STIGMA
+ STYLE

PISTIL

ANTHERS
+ FILAMENTS

STAMENS

MANGROVES, SWAMPS, GRASSLANDS, AND MOUNTAINS

The southern and southeastern United States encompasses Louisiana, Arkansas, Mississippi, Tennessee, Alabama, Georgia, Florida, South Carolina, North Carolina, Virginia, and West Virginia. It includes some of the most diverse and striking landscapes in North America. Starting out in the humid, subtropical climate of southern Florida, the coastal mangroves, cypress swamps, and tropical hardwood hammocks offer a bounty of different native plant communities. Heading north through the Southeastern Coastal Plain, this low-lying region from Louisiana to eastern Virginia harbors tremendous biodiversity and a multitude of distinctive habitats from maritime forests and bottomland swamps to wet prairies and longleaf pine woodlands. Moving farther northward, the low rolling plateau of the Piedmont is a narrow yet geologically complex region, with elevations extending over 1,000 feet above sea level. Lakes, rivers, and ravines are common in these foothills, as are oak-hickory-pine forests and mixed-deciduous forests. Continuing northward, the majestic Southern Appalachian Mountains are unmistakable. Formed some 300 million years ago, they run in an elongated band from northern Alabama northeast to eastern West Virginia and western Virginia, and feature a highly varied topography, including the highest point in the United States east of the Mississippi River at Mount Mitchell, North Carolina. The area includes crashing waterfalls, unspoiled old-growth forests, and high-elevation grassy balds with 360-degree views of the surrounding vast landscapes. Perhaps most impressive, however, is the fact that these mountains are among the biologically richest temperate areas in the world. Collectively, this region offers a dazzling assortment of wildflowers to enjoy.

Asclepias tuberosa

Butterflyweed
Height 1–2 feet; narrow, oblong leaves; flat terminal clusters; reddish-orange flowers

Bidens laevis

Smooth Beggartick
Height to 3 feet; toothed, shiny, lance-shape leaves; yellow flowers with brown center

Chamaecrista fasciculata

Partridge Pea
Height to 3 feet; ferny compound leaves; irregular yellow flowers with 5 petals

Chrysopsis mariana

Maryland Goldenaster
Height to 3 feet; hairy, oblong leaves; terminal clusters of yellow, daisy-like flowers

Conopholis americana

American Cancer-root
Height to 8 inches; leaves reduced to pointed oval scales; pinecone-like spike of flowers

Coreopsis basalis

Goldenmane Tickseed
Height 1–2 feet; deeply lobed compound leaves; golden flowers with dark brownish centers

Coreopsis lanceolata

Lanceleaf Coreopsis
Height 1–2 feet; entire to deeply lobed leaves; golden, daisy-like flowers atop erect green stems

Coreopsis leavenworthii

Leavensworth's Coreopsis
Height to 3 feet; linear, often lobed leaves; golden daisy-like flowers with notched petals and dark centers

Crotalaria rotundifolia

Crotalaria spectabilis

Rabbitbells
Height to 6 inches but often trailing to 2 feet; oval leaves; small, pea-like yellow flowers

Showy Rattlebox
Height to 6 feet; large oval leaves widest toward the tip; long spike of yellow, pea-like flowers; invasive

Cypripedium parviflorum

Gaillardia pulchella

Lesser Yellow Lady's Slipper
Height to 2.5 feet; broad leaves with parallel veins; 1–2 yellow flowers with 3 twisted petals

Indian Blanket
Height 1–2 feet; entire to toothed basal leaves; red-orange flowers with yellow-tipped petals

Gelsemium sempervirens

Helianthus angustifolius

Carolina Jessamine
Evergreen vine; height to 35 feet; glossy lance-shape leaves; yellow trumpet-shape flowers

Swamp Sunflower
Height to 8 feet; linear to lance-shape leaves; large yellow daisy-like flowers

Helianthus strumosus

Hemerocallis fulva

Paleleaf Woodland Sunflower
Height to 7 feet; slightly toothed lance-shape leaves; large yellow daisy-like flowers

Orange Daylily
Height to 5 feet; long, sword-like arching leaves; large, funnel-shape orange flowers marked with yellow

Hypericum hypericoides

St. Andrew's Cross
Height to 3 feet; small oval bluish-green leaves; small yellow flowers form an "X" shape

Hypoxis hirsuta

Common Goldstar
Height to 1 foot; linear, grass-like leaves; small, star-shape yellow flowers

Impatiens capensis

Jewelweed
Height to 5 feet; toothed, oval leaves on succulent stems; dangling horn-shape orange flowers

Lilium michauxii

Carolina Lily
Height to 3 feet; elliptical whorled leaves; nodding orange flowers with six recurved petals

Nuphar lutea

Yellow Pond-lily
Height to 3 feet; large flat heart-shape leaves; large cup-shape yellow flowers; aquatic

Oenothera biennis

Common Evening Primrose
Height to 7 feet; long lance-shape leaves; terminal spike of four petaled bright yellow flowers

Oenothera laciniata

Cutleaf Evening Primrose
Height to 1½ feet; deeply lobed oblong to elliptical leaves; yellow flowers with four heart-shape petals

Opuntia humifusa

Eastern Prickly Pear
Height to 2 feet; fleshy oval pads with numerous sharp bristles; large, waxy-looking yellow flowers; a cactus

Packera anonyma

Small's Ragwort
Height to 2 feet; long, toothed basal leaves; stem leaves lobed; clusters of small yellow flowers

Packera aurea

Golden Ragwort
Height to 2½ feet; heart-shape basal leaves; ferny stem leaves; clustered small yellow flowers

Platanthera ciliaris

Yellow Fringed Orchid
Height to 3 feet; lance-shape leaves; elongated cluster of orange to yellow-fringed flowers

Polygala lutea

Orange Milkwort
Height to 6 inches; oblong, somewhat succulent leaves; small spike of deep orange flowers

Pyrrhopappus carolinianus

Carolina Desert-chicory
Height to 3 feet; long, deeply lobed basal leaves; dandelion-like flowerheads on long stalk

Rudbeckia hirta

Black-eyed Susan
Height to 3 feet; toothed, oblong to lance-shape leaves; yellow daisy-like flowers with dark center

Senna marilandica

Maryland Senna
Height to 6 feet; long, compound, ferny leaves; clusters of yellow, pea-like flowers

Sida rhombifolia

Cuban Jute
Height to 3 feet; rhombus-shape leaves; pale yellow pinwheel-shape flowers

Solidago altissima

Uvularia grandiflora

Canada Goldenrod
Height to 6 feet; toothed, lance-shape leaves; plume-shape clusters of small yellow flowers

Largeflower Bellwort
Height to 2 feet; elliptical to lance-shape drooping leaves; bell-shape yellow flowers with twisted petals

Verbascum thapsus

Verbesina alternifolia

Common Mullein
Height to 7 feet; oblong downy leaves that get smaller up the stem; spike of yellow flowers

Wingstem
Height to 8 feet; toothed, elliptical to lance-shape leaves on winged stems; greenish-yellow, daisy-like flowers

Xyris torta

Slender Yelloweyed Grass
Height to 3 feet; long, grass-like green leaves; rounded heads of small yellow flowers below scale-like brown bracts

Agalinis purpurea

Purple False Foxglove
Height to 2½ feet; smooth, linear leaves; tubular lavender flowers with fine spreading lobes

Aquilegia canadensis

Red Columbine
Height to 3 feet; compound, lobed leaves; red and yellow nodding flowers with long spurs

Asclepias humistrata

Pinewoods Milkweed
Height to 2 feet; large oblong, leaves with pink veins; loose clusters of light pink flowers

Asclepias incarnata

Swamp Milkweed
Height 3–5 feet; narrow, lance-shape leaves; flat terminal clusters of pink-to-rose flowers

Asclepias syriaca

Common Milkweed
Height 2–6 feet; large, broad oblong leaves; rounded clusters of lavender flowers

Cirsium horridulum

Yellow Thistle
Height to 5 feet; basal rosette of dissected, spiny leaves; domed purple to whitish flower heads

Cypripedium acaule

Pink Lady's Slipper
Height to 18 inches; two elliptical basal leaves with parallel veins; single mauve, pouch-shape flower with flaring petals

Erythrina herbacea

Coralbean
Height to 6 feet; glossy, compound leaves with arrowhead-shape leaflets; elongated spike of bright red, tubular flowers

Trumpetweed

Height to 7 feet; whorled, toothed lance-shape leaves; large clusters of fuzzy pink flowers

Eastern Milkpea

Length to 4 feet; compound leaves with three oval to elliptical leaflets; clusters of pink flowers

Carolina Geranium

Height to 1 feet; deeply lobed, palm-shape leaves; 5-petaled white to pale pink flowers

Spotted Geranium

Height to 2½ feet; deeply lobed, palm-shape leaves; small 5-petaled lavender flowers

Cypressvine

Length to 20 feet; compound ferny leaves; trumpet-shape red flowers with five pointed lobes

Bayhops

Length to 30 feet; rounded leaves with a notched tip; funnel-shaped pink flowers with a darker throat

Mountain Laurel

Height to 10 feet; thick glossy elliptical leaves; clusters of white to light pink cup-shape flowers with purple markings

Henbit Deadnettle

Height to 1 feet; small, palm-shape lobed green leaves; whorls of lavender two-lipped tubular flowers

Red to Pink

Cardinal Flower
Height to 5 feet; lance-shape leaves; terminal spike of bright-red, lobed, tubular flowers

Trumpet Honeysuckle
Length to 15 feet; smooth, oval leaves; clusters of long tubular coral-red flowers

Powderpuff
Height to 8 inches; compound ferny leaves with linear leaflets; cluster of small pink flowers

Dotted Horsemint
Height to 3 feet; toothed, lance-shape leaves; tubular yellow flowers above colored bracts

Showy Evening Primrose
Height to 2 feet; lance-shape leaves; pink cup-shape flowers with four rounded petals

Turkey Tangle Frogfruit
Height to 8 inches; oval leaves; matchstick-like heads of purple flowers with a yellow throat

Maryland Meadowbeauty
Height to 2½ feet; serrated, lance-shape leaves; four-petaled white, pink, to rose flowers with yellow anthers

Mountain Azalea
Height to 15 feet; oval to elliptical leaves; clusters of funnel-shape pinkish flowers with long stamens

Catawba Rosebay
Height to 10 feet; shiny, evergreen, oblong leaves; round clusters of pink to lavender flowers

Carolina Rose
Height to 5 feet; compound leaves with 5-7 leaflets; 5-petaled pink flowers with yellow stamens

Rosepink
Height to 3 feet; clasping leaves; clusters of 5-petaled pink flowers with a yellow star-like center

Fire Pink
Height to 2½ feet; lance-shape leaves; star-shape bright red flowers with 5 notched petals

Woodland Pinkroot
Height to 2 feet; paired lance-shape leaves; clusters of red flowers with 5 yellow lobes

Florida Hedgenettle
Height to 18 inches; oval to spade-shape leaves; clusters of tubular light pink flowers

Red Clover
Height to 2 feet; compound leaves with three oval leaflets marked with a pale chevron; cluster of small pink flowers

Texas Vervain
Height to 2½ feet; leaves variable; basal leaves spatula-shape and narrower up the stem; clusters of small lavender flowers

White to Green

Achillea millefolium

Common Yarrow
Height to 3 feet; dissected, fern-like leaves; clusters of small white flowers with yellow centers

Argemone albiflora

Bluestem Pricklypoppy
Height to 5 feet; deeply lobed, spiny leaves; white flowers with wavy petals and yellow centers

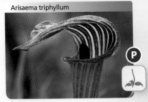
Arisaema triphyllum

Jack-in-the-Pulpit
Height to 2 feet; small spike inside leaf-like green and purple striped cylindrical sheath

Asclepias variegata

Redring Milkweed
Height to 3 feet; wide, wavy, oblong leaves; dense globular clusters of white flowers

Asclepias verticillata

Whorled Milkweed
Height to 3 feet; green linear leaves arranged in whorls; small flat clusters of whitish flowers

Baptisia alba

White Wild Indigo
Height 2–5 feet; compound clover-like leaves with three oblong leaflets; spikes of white flowers

Bidens alba

Spanish Needles
Height to 4 feet; compound leaves with 3 elliptical leaflets; yellow-centered white flowers

Ceanothus americanus

New Jersey Tea
Height to 3 feet; rough, toothed, oblong leaves; dense rounded clusters of small white flowers

White to Green

Cicuta maculata

Spotted Water Hemlock
Height to 6 feet; dissected doubly compound leaves; flat clusters of tiny, five-petaled, white flowers

Cnidoscolus stimulosus

Tread-softly
Height to 1½ feet; lobed, maple-like leaves with stinging spines; clusters of white flowers

Dalea pinnata

Summer Farewell
Height to 3 feet; compound leaves with needle-like leaflets; clusters of fuzzy white flowers

Daucus carota

Queen Anne's Lace
Height to 5 feet; compound, fern-like leaves; flat, lacy clusters of tiny, 5-petaled white flowers

Erigeron strigosus

Prairie Fleabane
Height to 3 feet; narrow elliptical leaves; clusters of small white, yellow-centered flowers

Eryngium yuccifolium

Rattlesnake Master
Height to 5 feet; narrow, strap-like leaves; small, rounded prickly heads of small white flowers

Euphorbia corollata

Flowering Spurge
Height to 3 feet; narrow oblong leaves; clusters of small white 5-petaled flowers with yellow centers

Euphorbia cyathophora

Fire on the Mountain
Height to 3 feet; elliptical to lobed, holly-shape leaves; clusters of small, inconspicuous flowers above partially red leaflike bracts

White to Green

Hibiscus moscheutos

Crimsoneyed Rosemallow
Height to 7 feet; toothed, large leaves; large pinkish-white flowers with a red center

Houstonia procumbens

Roundleaf Bluet
Height to 1 inch; small round to spade-shape leaves; small, tubular 4-lobed white flowers

Hydrangea quercifolia

Oakleaf Hydrangea
Height to 12 feet; large, heavily veined, oak-like leaves; large clusters of white flowers

Ipomoea pandurata

Man of the Earth
Length to 30 feet; big heart-shape leaves; clusters of 5-lobed white flowers with a purplish throat

Lachnanthes caroliniana

Carolina Redroot
Height to 3 feet; overlapping grass-like leaves; dome-like cluster of white-yellow flowers

Leucanthemum vulgare

Ox-eye Daisy
Height to 3 feet; lobed lance-shape leaves; flower with white petals around a yellow center

Maianthemum racemosum

False Solomon's Seal
Height to 3 feet; oblong to elliptical leaves; branched cluster of tiny cream-colored flowers

Melilotus alba

Sweetclover
Height to 8 feet; compound leaves with three oval leaflets; narrow spikes of small white flowers

White to Green

Climbing Hempvine
Length to 6 feet; heart-shape leaves; flat clusters of white flowers often with a pinkish hue

American Lotus
Height to 6 feet; large umbrella-shape leaves; cream flowers and a cone-shape center; aquatic

American White Waterlily
Height to 8 feet; large, deeply cleft round leaves; large yellow-centered white flowers

Mayapple
Height to 2 feet; one to two large palm-shape leaves; single nodding waxy white flower

Smooth Solomon's Seal
Height to 3 feet; large elliptical leaves with parallel veins; dangling clusters of bell-like cream flowers

Hoary Mountain Mint
Height to 4 feet; oval leaves; clusters small white to lavender flowers above white bracts

Narrowleaf Mountain Mint
Height to 3.5 feet; linear, needle-like leaves; dense ragged clusters of small purple-spotted lobed white flowers

Wild Radish
Height to 2½ feet; lobed, spatula-shape basal leaves, narrower stem leaves; loose cluster of white-to-yellow flowers

White to Green

Rhynchospora colorata

Starrush Whitetop
Height to 2 feet; grass-like basal leaves; clusters of small white flowers above white bracts

Rubus trivialis

Southern Dewberry
Height to 3 feet; heavily veined, glossy compound leaves; white 5-petaled flowers

Sagittaria latifolia

Broadleaf Arrowhead
Height to 3 feet; large arrow-shape leaves; 3-petaled white flowers and bright yellow centers

Saururus cernuus

Lizard's Tail
Height to 2½ feet; heart-shape green leaves; spikes of small white flowers curving downward

Stellaria pubera

Star Chickweed
Height to 1 feet; lance-shape to oval leaves; small starlike white flowers with red anthers

Symphyotrichum pilosum

Hairy White Oldfield Aster
Height to 5 feet; lance-shape to linear leaves; clusters of white flowers with yellow centers

Tephrosia virginiana

Goats' Rue
Height to 2 feet; compound, ferny leaves with oblong leaflets; clusters of cream-yellow and pink, pea-shape flowers

Thalictrum thalictroides

Rue Anemone
Height to 9 inches; oval 3-lobed leaves; loose clusters of white to pale pink flowers with many yellow anthers

White to Green

Tiarella cordifolia

Heartleaf Foamflower
Height to 1 foot; maple-shape leaves; long clusters of small white flowers with long stamens

Trillium grandiflorum

White Trillium
Height to 1½ feet; 3 large, broad oval leaves; single, large wavy white flower with yellow anthers

Verbesina virginica

White Crownbeard
Height to 6 feet; toothed, elliptical leaves; clusters of white flowers with a varying number of petals

Vicia caroliniana

Carolina Vetch
Height to 2 feet; compound ferny leaves with many oval leaflets; clusters of long, white flowers

Yucca filamentosa

Adam's Needle
Height to 8 feet; stiff, sword-shape basal leaves; clusters of cream-colored bell-shape flowers

Zephyranthes atamasca

Atamasco Lily
Height to 1 foot; long, grass-like leaves; large, trumpet-shape, 5-lobed white flowers that turn pinkish with age

Agalinis tenuifolia

Slenderleaf False Foxglove
Height to 2 feet; linear leaves; pink flowers with 5 rounded lobes and a white throat

Amsonia tabernaemontana

Eastern Bluestar
Height to 3 feet; elliptical to lance-shape smooth leaves; clusters of star-shape blue flowers

Centrosema virginianum

Spurred Butterfly Pea
Length to 8 feet; compound leaves with 3 elliptical leaflets; lavender flowers with a central keel

Clematis reticulata

Netleaf Leather Flower
Length to 10 feet or more; twice compound leaves with round leaflets; purple bell-shape flowers

Clitoria mariana

Atlantic Pigeonwings
Length to 4 feet; compound leaves with 3 leaflets; lavender flowers with a rounded bottom

Commelina erecta

Whitemouth Dayflower
Length to 3 feet; clasping leaves; flowers with 2 ear-like blue petals, a white petal, and yellow anthers

Conoclinium coelestinum

Blue Mistflower
Height 1–3 feet; triangular, veined leaves; flat clusters of fuzzy, light blue flowers

Dyschoriste oblongifolia

Oblong Twinflower
Height to 10 inches; oblong, hairy leaves; tubular, light purplish-blue flowers with 5 flaring lobes

Purple Coneflower

Height to 5 feet; coarse oval to lance-shape leaves; pink flowers around a raised, spiny center

Carolina Elephantsfoot

Height to 4 feet; elliptical, basal clasping leaves; clusters of small, tubular, white to lavender flowers

Showy Orchid

Height to 10 inches; 2 large basal leaves; flowers with curved pink hood and a long white lower lip

South American Mock Vervain

Height to 6 inches; small, ferny leaves; flat clusters of 5-petaled tubular, pink to lavender flowers

Azure Bluet

Height to 6 inches; small elliptical leaves; small 4-lobed pale blue flowers with yellow centers

Dwarf Violet Iris

Height to 6 inches; sword-like leaves that overlap at base; violet flowers with yellow patches

Virginia Iris

Height to 3 feet; long, sword-like leaves that overlap at the base; violet flowers with yellow patches and dark veining

Dense Blazing Star

Height to 4 feet; long, grass-like basal leaves; elongated dense spikes of small, tubular, pink flowers

Sundial Lupine
Height to 2 feet; palm-shape leaves with oblong leaflets; elongated spike of violet flowers

Virginia Bluebells
Height to 2 feet; large, smooth, oval leaves; clusters of tubular light blue, pendulous flowers

Lemon Bee Balm
Height to 2½ feet; aromatic, oblong leaves; clusters of lavender flowers above pink bracts

Wild Bergamot
Height to 4 feet; toothed, lance-shape leaves; clusters of pink flowers above leafy green bracts

Canada Toadflax
Height to 2 feet; smooth, linear leaves; spike of blue to violet flowers with a white throat

Violet Woodsorrel
Height to 15 inches; clover-like leaves with 3 heart-shape leaflets; clusters of bell-shape violet flowers

Purple Passionflower
Length to 20 feet; large, three-lobed maple-shape leaves; large, intricate lavender flowers with showy filaments

Canadian Lousewort
Height to 1 foot; oblong, lobed leaves; spike of two-lipped, tubular, yellow to reddish-brown flowers

Blue to Magenta

Phlox divaricata

Wild Blue Phlox
Height to 1½ feet; lance-shape hairy leaves; flat clusters of lilac to blue flowers

Phlox drummondii

Annual Phlox
Height 1–2 feet; lance-shape sticky leaves; clusters of 5-lobed red, pink, or white flowers

Pontederia cordata

Pickerelweed
Height to 3 feet; smooth, heart-shape leaves; long dense spike of violet-blue lobed flowers

Ruellia caroliniensis

Carolina Wild Petunia
Height to 3 feet; oval green leaves; small clusters of trumpet-shape 5-lobed purple flowers

Salvia azurea

Azure Blue Sage
Height to 5 feet; narrow lace-shape to oval leaves; loose spikes of tubular blue flowers

Salvia lyrata

Lyreleaf Sage
Height to 2 feet; basal rosette of lobed, lyre-shape leaves; spike of pale purple-blue, tubular flowers

Sisyrinchium angustifolium

Narrowleaf Blue-eyed Grass
Height to 2 feet; narrow, grass-like leaves; clusters of 6-petaled, blue to violet-blue, star-shape flowers with a yellow throat

Symphyotrichum laeve

Smooth Blue Aster
Height to 4 feet; toothed, lance-shape to oval, clasping leaves; clusters of violet to lavender flowers with yellow centers

Blue to Magenta

Ohio Spiderwort
Height 2–3 feet; grasslike leaves; clusters of 3-petaled blue-violet flowers with yellow anthers

Forked Bluecurls
Height to 3 feet; oval leaves; clusters of small violet-blue flowers with long, curved stamens

Clasping Venus' Looking Glass
Height to 1 foot; smooth, heart-shape clasping leaves; purple star-shape flowers

Brazilian Vervain
Height to 7 feet; serrated elliptical leaves; dense clusters of small lavender 5-petaled flowers

Giant Ironweed
Height to 8 feet; serrated lance-shape leaves; flat clusters of fuzzy magenta-purple flowers

Garden Vetch
Height to 2½ feet; compound leaves with up to 6 pairs of leaflets; small pinkish-purple flowers

Common Blue Violet
Height 3–8 inches; serrated heart-shape leaves; small violet-blue flowers with 5 rounded petals and a pale center

American Wisteria
Length to 30 feet; compound leaves with 9–15 elliptical leaflets, elongated, dangling clusters of lavender to purple flowers

Photo Credits

Adventure Quick Guides

Wildflowers organized by color for quick and easy identification

Simple and convenient—narrow your choices by color and leaf attachment, and view just a few wildflowers at a time

- Pocket-size format—easier than laminated foldouts

- Professional photos of flowers in bloom

- Similar colors grouped together to ensure that you quickly find what you're looking for

- Leaf icons for comparison and identification

- Easy-to-use information for even casual observers

- Expert author who is an entomologist and nature photographer

Get these *Adventure Quick Guides* for your area

NATURE / WILDFLOWERS / SOUTH / SOUTHEAST

ISBN 978-1-64755-133-9   **$9.95 U.S.**

5 0 9 9 5

Adventure
PUBLICATIONS
an imprint of AdventureKEEN

9 781647 551339